Black Women ar

Special Thanks

What would I do without my mother's touch, encouragement, patience and unconditional love. Mommie, you've been our rock, our shelter, our example of what it means to be a woman of integrity, a mother of infinite power, and a friend true and true. You continue to teach me lessons, which I humbly embrace. I am who I am because of you. You're my shero, mommie - I love you.

My sisters...laugh just thinking about you. We have so much fun when we're together. How mom managed to keep a straight face in public when we bust out laughing, just because, I have no idea. This book has been a long time coming. It's because of your ongoing support and applause that I, finally, stopped being afraid to succeed. I love you.

My babies...words are hard to come by when I think of you. I automatically smile really big, then I laugh, then tears of joy come to my eyes. I am so proud of you. You're the beat of my heart, the chill bumps on my arms, the smile on my face, the warmth of my soul. It's because of you that I live. Thank you, my loves. I love you.

My niece and nephew...the extension of my children. I breath with joy at the thought of you. Thank you for loving me unconditionally, for supporting me, for spending time just talking to me. Many thanks for educating me on the game of football and basketball, so I don't seem so clueless. Most of all, thank you for staying true to yourself. I love you.

Family…we all live so far away from each other, but we remain on each other's mind and in each other's lives. And when we do get together, we manage to pick right up where we left off. That makes me smile. That's the true essence of family – knowing that you are always home, always loved, and always supported. Thank you. I love you.

Friends…gotta have them. Friends play a special role in one's life – each having very specific responsibilities. Thanks to my friends for understanding your role and how very important you are to me. I am so thankful for your support, patience, and commitment to 'real' friendship. I love you.

Preface

Why are Black Women always so angry?' One evening, while I was channel flipping in hopes of finding a comedy, a documentary, a lecture about something positive – anything on the upswing, I heard those words, and that did it for me!

Is it the Truth, an Excuse or is it Something else? The purpose of this book of narrative, non-fictional articles promise to bitch slap you into owning your truth, then apologizing, forgiving, and hugging it out. It will enlighten, educate, answer that burning question that keeps so many up at night (smirk), and will help you help me help others who need help understanding the Truth, Excuse and the Something else as to why 'Black Women are always so angry'. Hmmmm.

Articles include:

Me and my Angry Black Mother which talks about my mother's struggle to beat the odds while living in the projects, on welfare, eligible for surplus cheese, married to a hustler, and how she single handedly confronted gang members on the weekend and worked in the Catholic School book store during the week. And mom has many secrets.

The Geo-Corporate Angry Black Woman with an Attitude - As Diversity Champion of a major corporate company, I hosted many events to support inclusion, but one exercise about Stereotypes is still being talked about 15 years later.

Why I love you so much. I love you so much because I can see it in your beautiful eyes – Your determination, your fight, your struggle, your perseverance. That spirit that measures your man-hood, that defies defeat - that spirit in which your mother's breasts nourished you for what's to come

Article's from an 'Angry' Black Woman

Truth, Excuse or Something else

Table of Contents

Black Women are 'ALWAYS' so angry

Before you get started, let me share with you what prompted me to write this book of articles -set the tone, if you will.

One evening, I was channel flipping - trying to find anything on TV that didn't include fighting, being hurt, being kidnapped, being killed, didn't involve shootings, children crying, nor women being disrespected. Ya know what I mean? As you can imagine, I damn near got carpel tunnel from channel flipping through all the drama. It's like looking in the refrigerator 3-4 times hoping that, magically, at next glance, you will find something that will satisfy your appetite. As I trekked through the channels, yet again, in hopes of finding a comedy, a documentary, a lecture about something positive – anything on the upswing, I heard it, **'Why are Black Women always so angry?'** That did it for me! I can't begin to tell you how tired I am of hearing this phrase spoken, as if it's true, so thought to write about it.

I decided to share my thoughts, my experiences and some facts in article format because I have much to say, but in different light, relative to the alleged Angry Black Woman.

First, as you're reading this book it's important that you stand in your truth. In other words, be honest about how you feel.

Throughout the various articles, I often use the word, 'society'. Because the word is ambiguous, for purposes of this book, I want to be clear about to whom I am referring when I use the word, society.

Society: If the shoe fits, I'm talking about you.

Second, when I use the words, 'blanket statement', it's in reference to stereotypes.

Third, if you have a conscious, you will read this book in its entirety. Then, forgive yourself for being part of the society in which I've defined earlier. Finally, simply embrace, except and honor our differences/similarities, and know better next time.

Article I – Truth, Excuse or Something Else

So let's get educated. **'Why are Black Women 'Always' so angry?' Truth, Excuse or is it Something else? Hmmmm.**

Fact: Hold onto your seat because this one is a doozy! Black women are NOT always so angry - black women carry centuries of HURT... HUGE difference. We're hurt because our hair, our body parts, our complexion, our intelligence, our walk, our talk, and our presence is often scrutinized - most of which is based on the negative perception that society has brainwashed us, yes, including me (in my younger years), into believing.

Society's Perception: My hair is too kinky, my skin is too dark, my ass is too big, my shape is too curvy, my lips are too big, my walk is too butch, my posture is too sloppy, my talk is too rough, my appearance is inferior, my presence is annoying, my attitude sucks, I'm aggressive, I'm loud, I'm rude, I'm unattractive, I don't know how to act in public, I'm embarrassing. I don't measure up, I don't look like..., I don't have..., Black women are always so angry. **That's a heavy load to carry, huh?**

Question: **Now, just for giggles, let's flip the script**. For my sista from another mista, and my brotha from another mutha, How would it make you feel if society constantly made those blanket statements about you? **Stand in your truth, please.**

Something to ponder: Like a child, who is constantly criticized, he/she begins to believe that about him/herself, and as a result, tries to 'change' in order to 'fit in', to be accepted, to please, to be loved. Oh, and yes, at times, becomes 'angry' because he/she can no longer be who he/she is, but rather must conform **in hopes of being accepted**. And, for my sista/mista, brotha/mutha who may not consider yourself a part of society, **STOP** and take a closer look. Perhaps your thoughts and/or actions come in different forms yet still translate to you feeling superior, privileged, entitled. That, or perhaps you're simply in denial. Call it what you will friend, but trust - you've lived a more 'acceptable' life, and that's the truth. **Keep reading, you'll relate to what I'm saying.** That is, if you're honest with yourself.

Truth: Psychologist and other therapist will tell you, time and time again, that, beneath ones anger, there is underlying, associated pain.

Excuse: OK, here it is, society....I'm not asking you to reveal your truth out loud, but rather to be honest with yourself as you read on. Because it makes society feel better about themselves by putting others down, and, in order to compensate for society's own behavior/choices, isn't it easier to blame it on the 'Angry Black Woman'?

Ha, I bet you think I'm angry as I share these thoughts. I even bet that you thought that I was going to go on this, 'White Woman, Black Man' kick.....wroooong. Instead, here's my response to that – You love who you love. **If you like it, I love it! If you love it, I'm all for it!** I'm just asking you to please don't use the 'Black Women are Always to Angry' thing as an excuse for your thoughts, actions and choices. Simply own your reason/excuse/logic/feeling and go with it.

Something else: **Here's where I dare you to open your eyes and your heart. It won't hurt – I promise.** WE WANT WHAT YOU WANT...to be loved....it's really that simple!! The word, love, encompasses so many things – Accepted, respected, embraced, adored, desired, appreciated....

Yes, we are a beautiful mess, but if you would open your eyes and truly look at us, I promise that you will be very impressed to see how our kinky hair, our big lips, our voluptuous asses, our beautiful shades of brown skin, how our intelligence, love, commitment, sacrifice, patience and blood, sweat and tears help shape this beautiful world in which we live. Show us some love, respect and acceptance, and we'll do the rest. We're naturally girls on fire(as Alisha Keys sings)!

OK, STOP! I can tell that some of you readers are getting defensive... your eye brows are all raised, your lips are poked out, your eyes wide-opened and some of you have even stopped breathing - all because you're feeling like I'm putting you on blast because you, ' don't think this way at all!' **EXACTLY!!** Just like you don't, necessarily, think that 'Black women are always so angry', see how it made you feel? A little offended; a little hurt, maybe ANGRY, huh? Calm down...Remember my definition of the word **Society – If the shoe fits, I'm talking about you.** Imagine how centuries of being cast as 'An Angry Black Woman' has affected us beautiful, gifted, loving, supportive, sacrificing, forgiving, fun-loving, happy, intelligent, daughter, sister, mother, grandmother, wife, friend, mentor, women.

Let me lighten the mood and introduce myself.

Don't fit the script – But I am an artist, damn it!

They say I don't look like an artist-

what the hell does that mean?

Are my nails too long? Are my hands too clean?

Is it in my stride? Is it in my walk?

Is it what I say? Is it the way I talk?

Is it cause I'm from the projects of upstate New York?

So I had a few fights-

kicked a few asses...

Does that mean I don't look like a true artist?

Hey, I graduated with honors; got a degree.

Is that what it takes for you to accept me?

Oh, and I was a small time thief, vandalized my coaches car,

but I was also a hell of a...hell of a track star.

A Big Sister, computer programmer...

I'm on top of my game.

Still don't look like an artist? Well, that's a damn shame.

Don't know what an artist looks like, but get use to this face...

and ya betta learn to love me, cause I ain't going no place.

p.s. I love you

Article II - Me and my 'Angry' black mother

I'd like to take you on a short journey through my life in hopes that you will better understand me as a woman. A journey in which many beautiful, loving, proud, forgiving black women paved the way for me to be where I am today.

I was born on September 30, and raised in the projects of Upstate New York where I lived with both parents and two sisters. We were tough, talented and very intelligent kids with two-sided hearts. One side full of love, compassion and empathy; the other side cold and made of steel. Both sides were needed to survive in the projects known for its gangs, drugs, violence and a place where taxi drivers refused to enter, and the police only came during times of riot. But for me, it was a place where I became street smart, book smart, developed common sense and had lots of fun. We, first, lived in the high-rise, apt 5A where the elevators, often, got stuck between floors, so once we sound the alarm and someone opened the elevator door, we'd either have to climb up or jump down to get out. The other alternative was to walk up five flights of stairs which, often, meant that we had to endure the smell of Wild Irish Rose, Colt 45 malt liquor and vomit, step in somebody's piss, spit, broken glass and garbage, then, step over guys who were passed out in the stair well. This was necessary in order to work our way up the staircase, often in the dark, in hopes that the door was unlocked once we arrived on the 5th floor (else we'd have to go up/down to the next floor and around to the other stairwell then back up/down to the fifth floor to gain access. Then, we'd run to Apt 5A in order to avoid the fight going on in the hall or in Ms. Delores apartment, or before Ms. Johnson opened her door asking for something.

Although there was constant gun fire, gang fights, fights amongst family members, drug traffic and police raids, we were good girls.

My mom, the youngest of 15 children, **NEVER** displayed that of **an 'Angry Black Woman'** in our presence. What I do remember is that mom ALWAYS sat outside in the courtyard while we played. In fact, Ms. Estelle would send her kids out to play when she saw that mom was outside. Mom was very **respected** by gang members, by residents, by store owners, by school teachers and by crack heads and the like. She could walk to and from work, school, the store, anywhere without fear. Her back was had!

Mom was also **ALWAYS involved**. Every day, she walked us to school, then, walked to work. When she was not working at the drug store, she worked at the Catholic school that we attended. This helped to off-set the cost of tuition and would allow her to have credit on school supplies that were purchased in the school bookstore. She also **volunteered** at what was called, 'The Lounge' which was located in one of the other high-rise buildings and where she monitored/scheduled, who was next in line to play pool, ping-pong, bumper pool..., so that there would not be any arguments over who 'got next'. This also helped keep track of who had the equipment last (in the event it came up missing). In spite of moms long work hours, working at the school, and volunteering at the lounge, she **ALWAYS** found time to play with us. Mom had hair down to her ass. For **fun**, she would messy her hair like a monster and chase us around the house. My sisters and I would laugh uncontrollably, allowing her to catch and tickle us. Mom loved to bake from scratch, often, making a variety of cookies and jelly roles. Sound like an angry black woman to you?

Never an 'Angry Black Woman', every year during camp season, mom walked us across the bridge to a central location which allowed for camp access to two other housing projects in which we were all rivals. Mom would then walk home, by herself, after dropping not only my sisters and I off, but neighbor's children that were put in moms care to deliver to and from camp, safely.

I remember this one day, as we were walking through the field, there was a gang of kids with broken bottles, chains and poles warning of trouble. Not sure what was going to go down, mom told my sisters and me not to dare run and to stick close to her. She warned the other kids who were walking with us not to run until we got to the sidewalk, then for them to run for their lives! Thankfully, the kids who were walking with us made it to the top of the bridge that separated our housing project from theirs. This forced the gang to stop in their tracks, throw rocks and turn around -never messing with mom and us.

Stories of mom and the struggle, and how she could call on Snaky to protect her, call on the nuns for help, talk the building manager into sparing us from eviction, and her playing **hero** by jumping in the middle of a gang fight that was about to go down because my older sister and I were wanna-be members, it would make you LOL and cry even louder - in the end, you'd walk away loving and respecting mom with every cell of your being. To top it off, if you could see her long kinky hair, **beautiful** caramel brown skin, skinny frame, **beautiful** smile and **perfect** lips, **you'd see that she is love.**

Never an 'Angry Black Woman', mom **taught us** right from wrong, **showed us** incredible work ethic, **gave us** strong self-esteem, was and still is an incredible **role model** for living right, doing the right thing, forgiving, loving, getting involved and is responsible for the thick skin and strong back bone which each of us behold.

My father, on the other hand, was abandoned by his mother and left to be raised by his grandmother, aunt, and whomever else was available. Always in survival mode, my father was a man of the streets. Very **street smart**, very **intelligent,** and very well **connected**. My father taught us, directly and indirectly, how to survive. He warned us at a very young age that he didn't know shit about being a father, but was a hell-of-a **hustler**. And that he was. A hustler, drug dealer, a great story-teller (sounds better than liar), very good looking, great drummer, master chess player, chain smoker and, from what mom says, the life of the party. Daddy had that same two-sided heart. The rarely seen gentle side which allowed him to be fun and compassionate while the steel side forced him to be manipulating, forceful, intimidating and a **survivor** by any means.

As adults, my mom shared with us how often my father's family wanted her to leave daddy. Mom's family wanted her to come back to her home state. Still others who loved her wanted her to leave for our safety, but, as I learned, she couldn't because of me. Mom said that she could tell how much I loved my father, and she refused to put me in a position of choice, but says that she also knew that it would be a matter of time. She just needed to wait until I was older and could better understand. Perhaps an 'Angry Black woman', during some of these times, but ONLY at her circumstance for which I'm sure most would understand.

The stories and secrets that mom could tell would make for a great 'Tell all'; however, that is not the purpose of this book. The purpose of this book is to diminish society's stereotype about black women.

To complete this short bio about me and my 'angry' black mother, want to share a piece that I drew called, 'The Projects'.

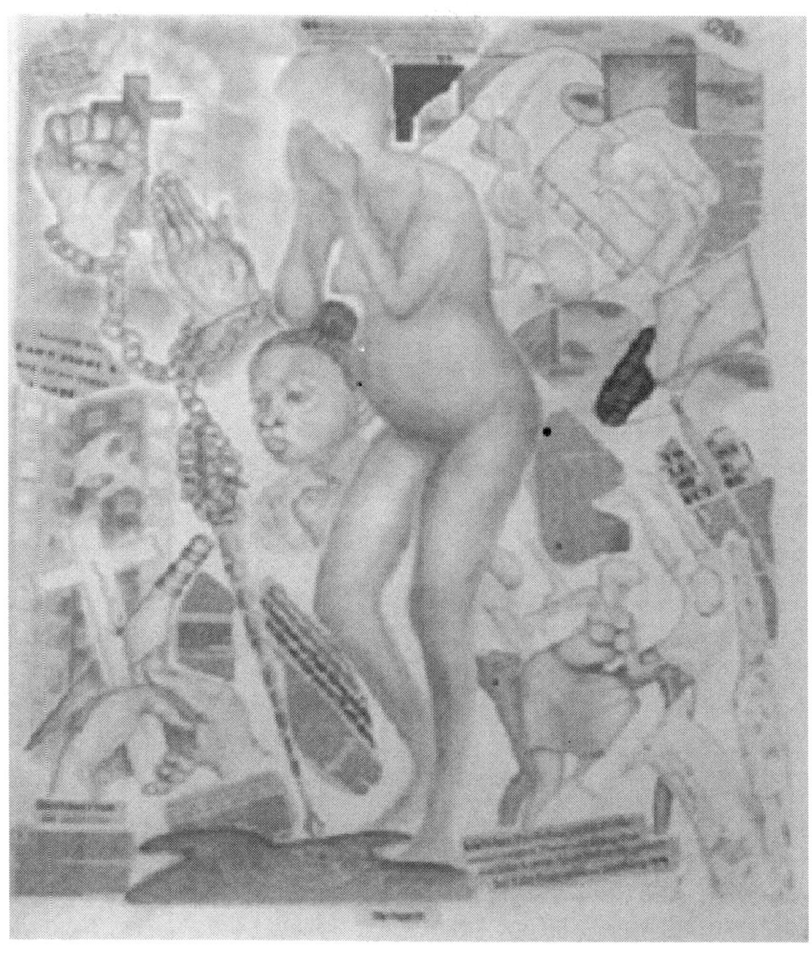

The Projects can be purchased on Webuyblack.com.

The Projects: The lady in the center of this piece represents my mother. Notice that she is pregnant. She cried every time she got pregnant, but not from lack of love for her unborn child, but because she didn't want to bring another child into her circumstance. The article above her head talks about secrets, **'Telling ones secret means that you have a strong sense of self and an ability to make peace with our past and move on'**. Now look at the two hands on the upper left side of the piece. Notice that the chain around the praying hand is loose. This depicts how easy it is to slip away from doing what is right in order to survive, while the chain around the hand making a fist is tight which reflects the struggle one faces, daily, so does whatever it takes to survive – Oppression dictates actions. The cross in the background says, **'We are obliged to Thank God even though events may challenge us – We are still standing**. The chain then connects to what represents a Knife and a syringe for which was a constant. And the puddle represents drugs and blood-shed. Notice that there is only one face in the entire piece. This face represents the struggle – oppression. This girl is only 9 years old. Her brother was killed in front of this high-rise building. Her mother, a very religious lady, struggled to believe in God after the killing of her son, thus, the knife penetrating the cross in front of the building. Notice the cutout in the building. This is reflective of the upper right hand side of the piece which says that, even with all of the obstacles and adverse circumstances, when you look inside, you will find loving families with a father who is present**...God-fearing and family focused – An everlasting love**. There are future leaders who want to make a difference, who are very intelligent, who are in the pursuit of happiness and justice for all. Finally, the lower right side of the piece represents the Block Parties we use to have when everyone got together and, in spite of it all, celebrated each other. The associated article reads, **'When I feel happy, it's like cruise control. Nothing can take that away....I can achieve anything'.** The various articles on this mixed media piece offer a strong and emotional message that tells my story growing up in the Projects, so **Never judge a man by his shoes in a dark room.**

Although growing up in our circumstances made us tough, street smart and a product of our environment, so to speak, we were never, 'Angry Black females'. We excelled in school, were track stars, captain of the girls' basketball team, participated in school plays and were and are still kind.

Article III - The Geographic Angry Black Woman

Moving to the Midwest was a culture shock - having grown up in the projects of Upstate New York where my friends were mostly black and Puerto Rican. The nuns, priests, crossing guard, and many of the store owners; however, were of the white persuasion, but since they had always been there, we didn't notice that they were white.

Let's fast forward to my adult years where one is forced to acknowledge the depth of society's opinion. Corporate America is where I began to really recognize how I was viewed. Not only an Angry Black woman, but rather **An angry black woman 'with an attitude'**(this is outside of the obvious prejudice for which my story won't embark) . I quickly came to understand that my New York mentality automatically meant that I had an attitude. Touché since I've labeled people who live in the Midwest as being annoyingly too sensitive, so fair game. What I didn't expect; however, is that this label would be used as an **excuse** for the CHOICES that some of my black brothers and society made. This, or course, is **without even getting to know me.**

Listen, I can get along with anybody. I'm optimistic, and, OK, maybe you have to win me over because of my New York mentality, but eventually, you'd find that I am very approachable, a ride-or-die chick, generous and kind. Following my mother's teachings, my heart is very forgiving. Following my father's teachings, I approach with caution.

Now, back to my corporate experience. With a strong work ethic, eager to begin a career, and noting an opportunity to impact stereotypes, I volunteered to be the Diversity Champion in the local office of a major corporation for which I worked. One of several events that I organized included a very powerful exercise surrounding stereotypes which was geared toward forcing attendees to stand in their truth about how they feel when certain words were introduced.

The exercise

- Around the conference room walls, I placed several large sheets of paper. On each sheet, I listed words to describe a stereotype (each was covered to avoid a pre-read).
- After a brief lecture, everyone was asked to stand in front of any of the covered sheets.
- Before uncovering the sheets, I emphasized the importance of being honest about what group of people they felt the words described.
- Each participant was asked to visit and address each of the sheets.

It was incredible how quiet the room was, and how obviously uncomfortable some were after writing down the group of people for which each stereo type, in their opinion, described. The honesty was obvious and very much appreciated as the purpose of the exercise was to understand and discuss society's impact on our psyche. As you may have guessed, the stereotypes were confirmed. That being said, there were two sheets in which I wanted to focus for purposes of this article.

Here are some of the words included on **Sheet One: Gang member, welfare, food stamps, small time thief, unemployed, trouble-makers, likely to end up in jail.** Attendees described these characteristics as belonging to: Black women, black people, black males, Hispanics and poor white trash (these were the exact words).

The other sheet in which I'd like to focus included the words: **Most likely to succeed, Track star, computer programmer, honor student, volunteer, Big Sister, team captain**. Attendees described these characteristics as belonging to: White people, Indian people, Asians were thrown in there a few times, and Black males even made the cut.

Finally, I revealed another sheet of paper where, on the left side of the sheet, I included some of the adjectives listed on **Sheet one** (see previous paragraph).

In the center of the sheet I placed a plus sign **(+)**. On the right side of the paper included some of the adjectives listed on **the other sheet** (see previous paragraph) , and underneath I placed an equal sign **(=)** and the word **ME**.

Imagine the surprised looks on the faces of most participants to learn that I was a gang member, who lived on welfare, and was a small time thief, and was also a track star, team captain, honor row student, and a Big Sister volunteer who graduated with a degree in Computer Technology and worked as a programmer.

Without further discussion, I encouraged the attendees to think about stereotypes, and how it creates division and limits acceptance. Then, I ended the session. And, yes, while there were some Angry Black Women in the room after seeing the only category in which they were placed, the session ended with a smile, a wink and a Thank You from each of them. Very clearly they were hurt, but I could also see their beautiful soul.

I dare my sistas/mistas and brotha/mutha to recognize that our beautiful hair, our luscious big lips, our big butts, our beautiful shades of brown skin, and how our intelligence, love, commitment, sacrifice, patience and blood, sweat and tears contribute to this beautiful world in which we all live – together. **We're naturally girls on fire!**(as Alisha Keys sings), AND, not so angry.

I AM

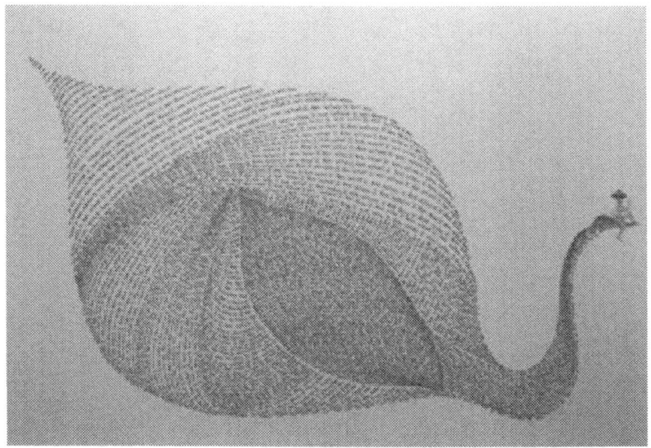

This BEAUTIFUL Swan is filled in with the following words that are repeated throughout to complete this vision of beauty: 'I am who I am, what I am, where I am, how I am, when I am....' The lady sitting on the beak of the swan is holding up her middle finger as if to say, 'Deal with it'.

Article IV – It takes a Pimp to Know One

What I find both funny and annoying about being labeled, 'An Angry Black Woman' is that, people, in general, have a bad habit of taking a phrase/excuse/an event and fitting it into their lives when it benefits them. Like anything, after continuous use, it becomes habit/mainstream/the norm.

As I continue to share my thoughts with you, I suddenly burst out laughing. Guess what?! **We're all pimps, yo!!!** In other words, we all have a way of controlling what people believe, wear, eat, say, buy...! Then, like a pimp, we use one's vulnerability for self-gain.

We can sell a pet rock, convince people that Orange is the new Black, persuade others that, if you put a smile in your voice, the receiver will believe you care; if you go in the 'wrong' neighborhood, you'll be robbed; if you wear Tom Ford, you've arrived; if you wear Chanel #5, the men will flock all over you;, if you marry rich and love later, you'll be happy....I can go on and on! Everybody's got game!! The question is, how do you use it? **What do you see when you look in the mirror – truth, excuse or something else?**

Let's take a closer look at the phrase, 'Black Women are Always so angry'. Virtually, every day that I turn on the TV and channel flip, there are 'Housewives' of all colors, nationalities and social status... and guess what –

They're often angry!!! Then, damn if I don't flip the channel and hear someone ask: 'Why are Black Women Always so Angry!' **And**, to top it off, there was a show that followed where a so called 'Angry' Black Woman was in the process of coming face to face with her anger because she has been convinced that, in deed, her constant anger is why her man now dates a sista/mista! Hmmm, **truth, excuse or something else?!!** I should mention that this show was not geared toward one Angry Black woman, but rather a group of 'Angry Black Women'!! What's really sad, is that these beautiful black women have been pimped into believing that they are truly 'always angry' and need to be 'fixed'. So, my question, **who pimped society into believing that Black Women are Always so Angry?**

If you(society) would stop using this stereotype as an excuse for **choices you make,** you'd sleep better, love harder, live happier. Om jus say'n.

Article V – Six Degrees from knowing who I am

You may be familiar with the theory around Six Degrees of Separation that was originally set out by Frigyes Karinthy in 1929 and which is defined in whatis.techtarget.com as “the theory that any person on the planet can be connected to any other person on the planet through a chain of acquaintances that has no more than five intermediaries”.[1] So, according to the article in whatis.techtarget.com, a chain of ‘**a friend of a friend**’ statement can be made to connect any two people in a maximum of six steps. This also complements the phrase, ‘It’s **a small world**’. Indeed it is. Society, **have we met?**

Sometimes, I sit and people watch – wondering where they’re going, wondering what’s going on in their life, wondering if they even notice me. I’m the girl who grew up in the projects of Upstate New York, who was a wanna be gang member, who had a few fights, was a Big Sister, who graduated with honors , was a computer programmer, traveled to a few places....yadda, yadda, yadda. And yes, I too have quoted the phrase, ‘it’s a small world’ a few times after meeting somebody who knows somebody, who knows somebody, who can help

---

[1] Whatis.techtarget.com, Posted by Margaret Rouse, *‘Six degrees of separation’* February 2007. TechTarget>whatis>definition>six-degrees-of-separation

me reach somebody – that's cute in all, but hmmmm, does this theory happen on a continuum or are we limited by fear of being open-minded or by chance?

Now that you've read this article, are you six degrees away from knowing who I am? What's the qualifier? **I DARE YOU TO FIND ME.** Trust, I'm not an 'Angry Black Woman'.

WHO ARE YOU - AM I?

Who are all these people…most of whom I've never met?

Are they future friends?

Will they come into my life eventually…

For a reason, a season, a life time?

Or, do I know all there is to know about them?

Do they wonder the same about me?

Are we all moving too fast to even notice on another?

I think that mother earth, father time, and life's got a hold on us all

Stop, breath, listen, feel, taste…I'm over here.

Article VI - Why I Love you so much

I love you so much because I can see it in your beautiful eyes – Your determination, your fight, your struggle, your perseverance. Your beautiful, strong, chocolate facial features tell the story of the plight of your beautiful ancestors who were born by the river praying that change is gonna come, and that you would see the grass on the other side, once you get over. The spirit of your great, great grandfather resonates to the deepest part of your core. You have that spirit that gives you the courage to withstand all obstacles. That spirit that measures your man-hood, that defies defeat - that spirit in which your mother's breasts nourished you for what's to come. Your eyes tell about the passion you have for family.

I watch in awe of your bravery every day that you leave home wearing a mask to conform to what society has defined as 'acceptable' in hopes that, today, you will overcome. You don't show your fear - determined to make it in this world, hoping that society will notice your contributions, begging quietly to be heard and to be given a chance, and praying that you'll make it home alive. **I fall in love with you over and over again** when I see the pain in your eyes, frustrated that you have to work twice as hard to get a nod - having to pat your own self on the back when you know that recognition is due. Watching you cry inside as you fight to be the man in which your ancestors paved the way.

My heart bursts at the thought of your strength. I admire your endurance, humility and humble spirit - taking pride as a blue color worker, a white color worker, a service provider, an entrepreneur, a manager, The President of the United States of America!

Tell me, how can I possibly be an angry black woman when I love you so much? I even love you as I sit on the park bench, and watch as you walk by, hand-n-hand with my sista from another mista, purposefully, making an effort not to look in my direction. I love you when you show your affection in public to my sista/mista, and even when you allow her to bitch slap me with her eyes and smirk as she side-eyes me before reaffirming that you're with her. Hey, you love who you love, and all I ask is that you stop using, 'Black Women are Always so Angry' as your excuse to justify your choices. **If you like it, I love it! If you love it, I'm all for it. Just own it and keep it moving!**

We beautiful black sistas love hard. We're not 'Always' angry – there's too much about us to love.

I'm in Love with my Sexy

I'm in love with my sexy; I'm in love with my funk,

I'm in love with my non-GMO anatomy; I'm in love with my mind, body and soul.

You know me as a woman, a sister, my mother's child, but you should watch me

as I nourish the souls of my offspring, exposing them to life's never ending pleasures -

overshadowing the cons of micro-peons of interruptible occurrences.

As I enter your space, I leave you a piece of my inspiration – what will you do with it?

Did you notice the energy in the air when I smiled at you? Did you feel your core explode in delight, exposing your soul as I walked by? Did you inhale my words of unconditional love?

I'm over here – stop, breath, feel my sexy.

Now, for you, my beautiful array of chocolate sistas. Don't think for a minute that I forgot about you. My love for you runs to the ends of the earth because I understand your heart. I understand how deeply you love; how committed you are to family; that when you do get angry, that it comes from feelings that you hold inside to keep the peace, to hide the hurt, to mask the struggle. But, when you smile, the whole world dances.

You, too, have that spirit that gives you the courage to withstand all obstacles. You behold that spirit that measures your woman-hood, and defies defeat - that spirit in which your mother's breasts nourished you for what's to come. Your eyes tell about the passion you have for family.

I watch in awe of your bravery every day that you leave home wearing a mask to conform to what society has defined as 'acceptable' in hopes that, today, you will be accepted. You don't show your fear, determined to make it in this world, hoping that society will notice your contributions, begging quietly to be heard and to be given a chance. **I fall in love with you over and over again** when I see the pain in your eyes, frustrated that you have to work twice as hard to get a nod - having to pat yourself on the back when you know that recognition is due. Watching you cry inside as you fight to be the woman in which your ancestors paved the way.

I smile as I type these next few thoughts because I am so in love with you – even when you don't give me the same welcoming greeting and smile that you give my sista from another mista who is standing in front of me in the grocery line. Even when I have a question and approach you with a smile, as you stand behind the airport counter, I still love you when you make me feel like I'm bothering you for asking for my assigned seat. My beautiful array of chocolate, I even love you when you are determined not to make eye contact with me as we pass each other on the street, BUT, haha, **I can tell that you appreciate the gesture and acknowledge the sediment as your peripheral vision captures my efforts.** And, it didn't even hurt. Let's make a pledge to honor our love every time we meet. I know you're not angry.

Believe me black beauty, I know that you're not displaying that of an Angry Black Woman. Our confidence has been(was once) shattered by society's betrayal of our soul. We have all fallen victim(pimped) to the stereotype that has been cast, branded and subconsciously imputed so deep into our soul that we have been made to believe it to be so. The next time you look in the mirror, look into your eyes and see love. See all of the women who paved the way for us to be where we are today and stand tall, stand proud, stand beautiful. Proudly show those curvy hips, those beautiful lips, that amazing kinky hair, that brown skin. Then, look to the right at my sista/mista and notice how she has spent thousands of dollars altering her body to mimic our beautiful features and hue. Then, smile even bigger, acknowledging their efforts... maybe even wink, then walk on by, gracefully.

Article VII – Black Love and the Family Dynamic

Sure, outwardly, at times, I display that of an Angry Black Woman because society has shit on me once too many times, but I have, finally, learned to lift my head, pick my afro, love my lips, accept my hips, and oil my beautiful black skin so it shimmers in delight while looking society straight in the eye and say, **'It's not me, it's you!'** Very proud to say that I, no longer, own your issues, but rather recognize your obsession with me. Try, acceptance...I hear love goes a long way, too! **Free at last - Thank GOD almighty, I am free at last!!**

Black Love and the Family Dynamic

40 Years, 7 days, 2 hours and a kiss
(special edition)

Fifty something going on sixteen –

That's the way he makes her feel.

All giggly and silly...puppylove-like, for real.

And when he sees her, you can see it in his eyes –

All giggy, side pimp'n, hand sweat'n, heart beat'n...

All those emotions arise.

Three kids, 40 years, 7 days, 2 hours and a kiss –

And she still loves him like the first day they met.

And she…well, she's in his life for a reason, a season, AND a lifetime –

that you can bet.

Her phone has a special ring tone, just for him, that

when heard makes her blush.

It's the middle of the day! You just left him! Can a sista get some girlfriend time –

what's the rush?!!

But I know that when it comes to 'them', I need to just hush.

If you take a look at them, now,

at 40 years, 7 days, 2 hours and a kiss, you'd say,

'Wake up from that dream, fix those clothes, open those eyes –

Cause at 50 something, you don't want an "oops baby", anniversary surprise!!'

Don't know if there's any deeper love to be got –

Cause the depth of their love, we can all agree, baby, is

HOT, HOT, HOT!

Look at them at 40 years, 7 days, 2 hours and a kiss –

Fifty something going on sixteen.

Need I say more?

Article VIII - Census and the Angry Black Woman

So far, you've read seven Articles about the Black women from a Black woman. Considering the source, you can count on these experiences as being the Truth.

Now, before you get your panties all in a bunch and your balls all in a knot, let me speak to the word," angry", and its relationship to the Black woman as tagged by society. But before I do that, let's look at some definitions and Census.

According to Dictionary.com, Angry is defined as feeling or showing anger or strong resentment (usually followed by at, with, or about).

So, as we interject the definition of the word angry into the phrase as often quoted by society, 'Black Women are Always so Angry', let's take a peek at some stats from the US Census Bureau.

According to the US Census Bureau information found on BlackDemographics.com:[2]

- The black female population in the US was 23.5m in 2013. This is 52% of the total black population.

---

[2] BlackDemographics.com, *African American Women,* Population, Education, Employment, Other Characteristics

- 57% of black women 25 and older attended college compared to 60% of all women.
- 26% of black women have some college, compared to 21% of all women
- 9% of black women have an Associate's Degree compared to 9% of all women
- 28% of black women graduated from High School(or GED) compared to 27% of all women.
- Yet, 36% of black women who worked full time all year in 2014 had average earnings of $33,780 compared to $38,097 for all women. hmmmm

Impressive stats, huh, yet unequal concession, recognition, compassion, consideration, compensations... AND I never even got my reparation. Can you blame a sista for being angry? **But still I rise, I love, I forgive, I embrace – holding onto that stone of hope**.

Now, let's do the math without entering into a long drawn out formula, but rather concluding based on common sense. If black women were always so angry, can you imagine what their overall contribution would entail? **EXACTLY!!!!** The stats would not be as impressive, our contributions would not be as newsworthy and our truth would continue to be ignored.

Whatever your response, you were either able to confirm, identify with or be in opposition of - and you're absolutely right - it's NOT only Black Women! But, with love, the alleged 'Angry' Black woman is what this book is about, so there!

So, now it's time for a quick Pop Quiz

Quiz: **BE HONEST** (True/False)

1. I've never said/don't believe that black women are always so angry/mean.
2. I don't shun(look away) from black women when I approach them.
3. I have a preconceived opinion of black women in general.
4. I am just as friendly toward black women as I am toward anyone.
5. I often acknowledge a black woman's presence.
6. I respect black women.
7. I show black women genuine care.
8. I love black women.
9. I believe that black women are angry most of the time.
10. Other (explain):

    ____

____

____

There's no right or wrong answer, only your truth. Own your stuff. I own mine.

Article IX - Beauty and the Twenty-Dollar Bill

The Twenty-Dollar Bill! So there I was, channel flipping trying to find anything on TV that didn't include fighting, being hurt, being kidnapped or being killed, didn't involve shootings, children crying, nor women being disrespected. Carpel tunnel setting in from channel flipping through all the drama - like looking in the refrigerator 3-4 times, hoping that, at next glance, you will find something that will satisfy your appetite. I trekked back through the channels 3-4 times in hopes of finding a comedy, a documentary, a lecture about something positive when all of a sudden, I see a panel of women talking about the Twenty-Dollar bill. Intrigued, I sat back in my 23 year old, egg white, worn but comfy, oversized Italian leather, chair to get educated.

Lawd, here we go again! This time the conversation was not necessarily about an angry black woman, but rather a discussion about a beautiful black Civil Rights woman and what that means to the Twenty dollar bill. **Give me a break, already!** Somebody please help me wrap my mind around how a conversation can move from celebrating the bravery and heroism of this beautiful black woman to a conversation about whether or not she is pretty enough to adorn the Twenty-Dollar bill! No, I'm not an Angry Black Woman, I just don't get how society is continually given cart blanch to define beauty when it comes to the black woman! And as I listen to the array of brown women speak so eloquently about her – Thank you, I can't help but wonder WHY her looks are of concern. Hmmmm, were looks considered before putting my brotha's from anotha mutha on a bill?

While I appreciate the concept of gracing the Twenty-Dollar bill with this beautiful black woman who paid for me to be here, I can't help but wonder, 'did these same conversations take place before putting my sista's on a stamp? Yes, we've come a long way baby; we've seen the fruits of our labor in many ways; we continue to pave the way, to forgive, to love, to honor and cherish till death do us part, but **relationships are a two-way street, dam-it!**

Speaking of relationships, I will never forget listening to a discussion in which an audience spent time sharing their thoughts about what they think it takes to build a long, loving relationship. After a few minutes of opinion-sharing, a female senior citizen stood up and said, 'I have listened to this conversation long enough, and I can't take it anymore. She goes on to say that the problem with what everyone is saying all leads to 'change'. You thought you could change him/her. You thought that if he/she would just change his/her ways, your relationship would flourish.' She then points to her husband of sixty-eight years and says, 'Look at my husband. He's a slob! He was a slob before I met him, and sixty-eight years later, he's still a slob, but this man has loved me for the nag that I was before we got married and loves me for the nag that I am to this day. Why? **It's about acceptance.** If you all can accept each other for who he/she is, you will find ever-lasting love. And if you can't accept him/her for what you believe to be a shortcoming, walk away before you commit to investing your life in that relationship. People, it's about acceptance. Acceptance is powerful.' The audience was numb. Then, a standing ovation followed.

Acceptance! Now, there's a concept! How about we try some acceptance and watch hearts open, watch attitudes change, and stereotypes dissolve. Then, I bet that the conversation about the Twenty-Dollar bill would simply be, 'When do we put it into production.'

Article X - Almost There

I created an art piece that I call, 'Almost There'. As an artist, my work has no set direction, nor focus, but rather is often inspired by life experiences, day-dreaming, and aimless doodling. It ranges from serious depictions of strength, to clever portrayals of corporate slang, to metaphoric images that inspire thought, to simple lines that tell a story. What I love most about art is that the piece can change direction at any given time with just the slightest change in thought, a twist of the wrist, or a mood swing.

When I finished this piece that I created with no set direction, I stepped back and studied it for a while. I wasn't even sure in which direction the piece should land – each projecting a different meaning. After flipping, studying and walking away from the piece several times, I settled on what would be its final resting position. Smiling, I shook my head and recited, **'I know exactly where I'm going, it's just not in the direction you want me to go...Trust me, I'm almost there.**'

So, I have a question for you, Society, where are you going with this whole Black Women are Always so Angry, thing? Come on now -what's the point of labeling me as an Angry Black Woman? **I know exactly where I'm going.**

Pop Quiz – **Be Honest** (True/False)

- I care about what people think about me.
- I try to conform to the masses because I want to fit in.
- I think that I'm: (Circle all that apply)

Unattractive	Kind	Judgmental	Forgiving
OK looking	A follower	Confident	Opinionated
Beautiful	Optimistic	A leader	Open-minded

Now take another look in the mirror and say, '**Today is the first day of the rest of your life!'** 'I know exactly where I'm going, it's just not in the direction you want me to go...Trust me, I'm almost there.' Own your truth and stop blaming me.

Article XI - White Paper Black Ink, Color Pencils

As a non-angry black woman and artist, I see the beauty, the potential and the mystery in everything including the gray space. Take this white sheet of paper that started out blank. **The beauty** is that this blank piece of white paper was at my disposal to do with it as I will. **The potential** for this piece of white paper is that it can be folded, cut, decorated, or it can behold information that tells a story. **The mystery** of this blank piece of white paper is that, as it sits alone, one can only wonder what will become of it.

As you can see, the black ink is what brings this sheet of white paper to life. **The beauty** of the words give purpose to how the two will work hand-in-hand to spark interest. The black ink defines the space by offering wisdom with **the potential** of educating its readers about the angry black woman. The black ink solves **the mystery** of what really lies in the hearts of the angry black woman.

Where would this white sheet of paper be without this black ink? Where would this black ink be without this white paper?

Now, let's imagine what would happen if you mix in an array of color pencils. The Black ink is not threatened by the array of beautiful color pencils, but rather appreciates the complement. So, why can't the Angry Black woman catch a break? My beautiful black 'ink' brings dreams to life. I dare you to look beyond what society has you believing, and **look into the eyes of this angry black ink and see my soul**.

Article XII – Black night, Black sky, Black room & The Angry Black Woman

My skin - dark as the night – until the lights reveal my hue. **My face** - beautiful as the night sky, present in every episode of life. **My heart** - mysterious as a dark room until you open your heart and let me in. Like the black night, black sky and black room, if you don't open your mind and acknowledge that I'm not always so angry, and if you don't open your hearts and accept me for the beautiful mess that I am, you will continue to miss out on the essence of me and what we can be, together. Dark as the night, beautiful as the sky, and mysterious as a dark room - **not always an Angry Black Woman.**

Article XIII – With Love, from an Angry Black Women

From my heart: I'm somebody's daughter, sister, mother, grandmother, wife, friend, hero, mentor, and I'm crying – see me, hear me, respect me, love me. Because **I understand** that you've been brainwashed by society, because **I'm compassionate**, because I have a backbone that won't quit and because **I love you, I forgive** you every time that you say/think that 'Black Women are Always so Angry'

That I can smile while typing these words, tells you that I haven't given up on you. I'm not an 'Angry Black Woman'. I want to be respected and loved for the beautiful mess that I am - smart, loving, funny, silly, artistic, light hearted, optimistic, with kinky hair, brown skin, pudgy tummy, voluptuous ass, thick legs, and a beautiful soul.

Write the Last Article for me

I want to start a movement and invite you to write the final chapter. Sum up your thoughts in 15 words or less expressing your feelings after reading this book. **Everyone is welcome!** By **volunteering** to send me your thoughts, you are **giving me permission** to include them in the next series. Your submission waives any and all rights and claims that you might claim in relation to me, this book and any future books and/or endeavors by me. You understand that your submission is **strictly voluntary**.

To respect your privacy, please sign your thoughts as follows: If you're black, sign, 'Sista' or 'brotha'. If you're not black, sign, 'Sista/mista' or 'brotha/mutha'.

To make the final chapter authentic, I'd love to use your actual penmanship v. a typed version, but respect your preference should you decide on a typed response. Email your thoughts to, dashart@aol.com. So that I won't view your email as Spam/Junk, please put the words, '**Final Chapter'** in the subject line.

It's been a pleasure educating and sharing my thoughts and experiences with you.

Signed, Not at all, and Angry Black Woman☺

You're awesome! Thank you for reading, educating yourself, apologizing, and hugging it out with me. Now, let's move on!

Made in the USA
Middletown, DE
01 May 2017